The
Seven Deadly Sins

© Robert Chantler 2002, 2013

All rights reserved.

The author asserts his right to be identified as the creator of this work under the Copyright, Designs and Patents Act 1988.

Amateur dramatics societies do not have to pay royalties to perform this work as long as details of any performance are notified to the author and no alterations are made to the script without written permission.

Published by
The Free Theatre Company Press
Shepperton, Middlesex, UK

ISBN – 978 0 9561 352 9 2

GUIDANCE FOR SET DESIGNER

The counselling room should be neutrally decorated. The window is at the rear with hanging beige blinds. There are three comfortable chairs, with a central chair and both outer chairs at 45 degrees to each other. In the middle of the three is a small teak coffee table with a box of tissues on it. A pot plant sits next to the chair on the right. A small table with a coffee machine, teabags, kettle etc is next to the chair on the left. A rug is under the coffee table and extends beyond it to fill the floor space in between the three comfy chairs.

An external scenery drape is needed behind the window, which should be of a sash type that opens widely.

CHARACTERISATION

The cast should feel free to interpret the characters as they wish. The director need not be specific, except where, for example, an age / age range, size etc is stated.

AUDIENCE

The plays do contain adult themes, and innuendo as well as mild swearing and should not be shown to persons under the age of 12 years.

Robert Chantler – The Seven Deadly Sins

LUST

Caroline (Sex Therapist)
Warren and Samantha (Young couple)

Robert Chantler – The Seven Deadly Sins

LUST

(CAROLINE stands to welcome them and they all sit)

CAROLINE:
Do come in. It's very nice to meet you both. Warren isn't it?

WARREN:
Yes.

CAROLINE:
And Samantha.

WARREN:
Yes.

CAROLINE:
Make yourselves comfortable. Would you like a tea or coffee?

WARREN:
No thanks.

SAMANTHA:
Maybe later.

CAROLINE:
Okay. (pause) Now, how can I help you?

WARREN:
We can manage fine on our own thanks.

SAMANTHA:
About the situation darling, not the sex act.

WARREN:
Oh well. Our relationship is based purely on sex. 100% pure animal sex, know what I mean?

CAROLINE:
Shallow.

WARREN:
No, I mean passionate. Physical.

CAROLINE:
Yes, but surely there's more to a relationship than just sex?

WARREN:
Sorry, you are a sex therapist aren't you? With the emphasis on sex?

CAROLINE:
Of course, but I look at a relationship holistically. Anyway, if you have such good sex, do you really need my help?

WARREN:
Yes.

SAMANTHA:
You see, doctor, when a relationship relies so much on sex, when the sex loses it's magic, it's hard.

WARREN:
Magic or not, it's always hard.

SAMANTHA:
The relationship darling, not your cock.

WARREN:
Oh. Yeah, well. It's Samantha.

SAMANTHA:
(indignant) It's us. We've done it so often it's kind of…going through the motions. Nothing more.

CAROLINE:
Okay, so you have a purely physical relationship. Are you saying through that there's nothing there without the sex? You don't connect on any other level?

WARREN:
Not really. We had sex in different places, like the multi-storey.

SAMANTHA:

The roof level darling. In our Volvo.

WARREN:

Oh yeah. Then it failed its MOT on the suspension the following week. Do you remember?

SAMANTHA:

(smiles) Yeah.

CAROLINE:

I wonder why.

WARREN:

Great car. The seats go back a really long way!

SAMANTHA:

Lots of leg room.

CAROLINE:

Yes, but what concerns me is what is going to happen to the relationship when you're older and frailer. Maybe you won't be physically fit enough or look attractive enough to each other. What then?

WARREN:

Well, that's too far ahead doc. We don't think ahead like that. Live for the now, that's us.

SAMANTHA:

Yeah, we don't worry about what might happen when we get old. I might get knocked down by a bus tomorrow.

WARREN:

Yeah, who knows what's round the corner?

SAMANTHA:

Except more sex!

WARREN:

Exactly!

CAROLINE:

You know, the first step that seems to help couples in your position, em…situation, is to rekindle the desire. In other words, stop having sex.

WARREN:

What? (To SAMANTHA) Whose idea was it to see this quack!

SAMANTHA:

It was in Cosmo last month.

WARREN:

(sarcastically) Oh right, well it must be a good idea then!

CAROLINE:
Look, I want you to stop having sex so that you desire it more. Abstinence makes the feelings grow stronger, and when you do something less often, you enjoy it more when you do it. Set yourself a target. No sex for a month. Every time you feel the urge and beat it, reward yourselves.

SAMANTHA:
With sex! (pause) Oh no, that won't work will it.

WARREN:
We could watch a dirty movie.

SAMANTHA:
Not the same though. Hey, how about we go to Ann Summers and buy something sexy!

WARREN:
No, that won't work will it. We'd just be more lustful than ever.

SAMANTHA:
You see, we can't avoid sex. We just can't. Everything always comes back to sex.

CAROLINE:
Well, okay. How about you cook a nice romantic meal?

SAMANTHA:
Oh I'm not that good at cooking. Something simple I guess. A few candles, romantic music.

WARREN:
Toad in the hole!

SAMANTHA:
Yes, then afterwards we can have dinner! (pause) Oh, the menu.

WARREN:
What about dessert?

SAMANTHA:
Spotted dick, and…ooh, ice *cream*!

WARREN:
Oh yeah, it really turns me on when you do that. (pause) Oh, the menu.

SAMANTHA:
Shall we do it tonight?

WARREN:
Well, I thought we were going to try and last a month.

SAMANTHA:
I mean try the meal darling.

WARREN:
Oh yeah, right. Leave Mission Impossible, eh?

SAMANTHA:
Yeah.

CAROLINE:
My God, you two really are obsessed with sex aren't you.

WARREN:
You've finally got it! Glad all that book knowledge hasn't gone to waste! We can't not have sex. We're sexual compulsives! That's how we met, in group.

SAMANTHA:
Yes, so romantic. Remember when we first met?

WARREN:
(dreamily) Oh yes.

SAMANTHA:
(fondly) And you bought me that Rampant Rabbit.

WARREN:
(dirtily) Oh yeah. For when my personal rampant rabbit wasn't in the rabbit hole, which wasn't very often.

SAMANTHA:
No. (To CAROLINE) It was just for when he was at work really.

WARREN:
Yeah.

CAROLINE:
Well then, perhaps you should try some different sorts of sex. Different positions perhaps, or fantasy. Dress up a bit! You know the sort of thing I mean.

SAMANTHA:
I *have* got that maid's outfit.

WARREN:
I know but you often wear that. Not that it's not sexy, because it is. Ooh, I'm feeling all excited right now just thinking about it.

CAROLINE:
Something period would be romantic. Think how sexy you'd feel in a beautiful eighteenth century ball gown, bosoms under your chin, a tiny waist…

SAMANTHA:
To have sex in?

CAROLINE:
No, to set the mood. Then in comes Warren. "Take me you huge man!" you scream. "I'll tame you my lusty wench!" Warren shouts back!!

SAMANTHA:
(To WARREN) She's going to have a heart attack in a minute.

WARREN:
Calm down doc.

CAROLINE:
I get carried away sometimes. Sorry.

WARREN:
So you must have a good sex life then?

CAROLINE:
Oh fantastic. My sex therapist is brilliant.

WARREN:
You seeing a sex therapist!?

CAROLINE:
Of course.

WARREN:
Talk about the blind leading the blind.

CAROLINE:
No, all therapists have to see a therapist regularly. It is part of our requirements to practice.

SAMANTHA:
Weird.

CAROLINE:
Well, on the face of it, but it's good to have someone to bounce off.

WARREN:
Yeah, we do that.

CAROLINE:
Bounce ideas off, Warren.

WARREN:
Oh. Anyway, don't tell us we don't experiment. Have you ever tried to have sex when you and your partner are wearing giant inflatable sumo costumes?

CAROLINE:
No.

SAMANTHA:
It's fun. You're really pushing and pushing against each other but sex just doesn't happen!

WARREN:

(To CAROLINE) That's because my todger's inside the sumo cos…

CAROLINE:

Yes, thank you.

WARREN:

We normally just roll off the bed, and laugh a lot.

CAROLINE:

You see, you can have fun and be romantic without having sex.

WARREN:

Well, I was going to add, that when we finally get up, we strip off our sumo costumes and have sex!

CAROLINE:

Well, next time try the sumo thing without the sex at the end. Just to see what happens.

SAMANTHA:

Oh I know what will happen. We'll both be horny and restless all day.

CAROLINE:

What did you hope I would do for you?

WARREN:

Tell us how we can have loads of sex without getting bored of it and without having less of it.

CAROLINE:

Well, I can't do both.

SAMANTHA:

Well, you're not much use to us are you?

CAROLINE:

Okay, here's what I suggest. Many couples find that when they have too much sex it gets dull and they don't feel like doing it, and then they don't like that – that's the situation you're both in. The idea of denying yourself sex when you feel you want it, even if that denial stops a purely mechanical act is sound; the more times you deny yourself that act, the more you'll want it when you finally yield. That's option one. Option two is to spice it up a bit by any means you both consider feasible.

SAMANTHA:

That sounds very generic.

WARREN:

I bet you say that to all your couples.

CAROLINE:

Well, that's really all I have. If you don't have equipment problems and you're confident about having sex, it really just comes down to re-igniting that spark.

SAMANTHA:

Okay, we'll try.

WARREN:

Actually, I quite fancy some now.

SAMANTHA:

Yeah, me too! Get your clothes off – we'll do it on the floor right now!

WARREN:

Yeah!!

CAROLINE:

No, no, no!! No!!!

WARREN:

Just winding you up doc. (To AUDIENCE) I bet you're relieved too, eh?

CAROLINE:

(To WARREN) Yes, well, we've all had some fun there haven't we.

SAMANTHA:

But the fun never lasts does it. It's like a hit. You have a climax and then the drug wears off, so you have to have more. It's the same with sex – for us, anyway.

CAROLINE:

Well, I'm afraid our time is up. That'll be ninety pounds please.

SAMANTHA:

Ninety pounds!??!

CAROLINE:

That's what you get for indulging in lust. Emotional poverty, spiritual poverty and financial poverty.

WARREN:

Okay, I can see your point.

SAMANTHA:

One good thing about not having sex. At least I'll be able to walk properly.

CAROLINE:

Well, it was nice to lighten your load.

WARREN:

Yeah, I'm ninety quid lighter!!

SAMANTHA:

We will try to abstain, but I don't know how we'd cope.

WARREN:

Well, we could have an open relationship. Temporarily.

SAMANTHA:

What, see other people? Sleep around?

WARREN:

Yeah.

SAMANTHA:

Of course, if we're bored of each other we'll just have a few weeks having sex with total strangers!! Drunken one night stands. And then we can look back on hazy memories of sexual excesses in the weeks to come.

WARREN:

How romantic! (To CAROLINE) We want a refund please.

THE END

SLOTH

Richard (Life Coach)
Paul (Client)

Robert Chantler – The Seven Deadly Sins

SLOTH

RICHARD:

Paul? Paul Morris?

PAUL:

Yeah.

RICHARD:

Richard Hunter. Life Coach.

PAUL:

(swaggers in and flops into chair) Hi.

RICHARD:

Did you have a good journey?

PAUL:

Nah.

RICHARD:

Oh, I'm sorry to hear that. What happened then?

PAUL:

Nothing. Can't be bothered to talk about it.

RICHARD:
Okay, well I gather that you have been told that if don't get a job, you'll have your benefit stopped, correct?

PAUL:
Yeah.

RICHARD:
Having seen you so far, I'm surprised you even manage to haul yourself out of bed to go to the toilet.

PAUL:
It's a struggle, that's for sure.

RICHARD:
So what do you do all day?

PAUL:
Lie around. Got a mini fridge, water, tea and coffee maker, lager, fags, TV remote, stereo remote, radio, phone – all around my bed. Bathroom's next door to my room. Fine as long as Shelley don't keep me up all night throwing up ten pints.

RICHARD:
Shelley?

PAUL:
My partner.

RICHARD:
Does she work?

PAUL:
Nah.

RICHARD:
And is her benefit being stopped?

PAUL:
Nah. She gets loads, child support and stuff like that.

RICHARD:
You have a child. You actually had the energy to have sex?!

PAUL:
Well I just lay there, she did most of the work.

RICHARD:
But you pulled it off.

PAUL:
Well, she did.

RICHARD:
What sort of father do you think you are?

PAUL:
A bad one?

RICHARD:
I think many people would say that, yes.

PAUL:
And you?

RICHARD:
I'm not here to judge you. I'm here to help you judge yourself, realise your situation is now untenable and feel genuinely motivated to change for the better.

PAUL:
Shorter words, mate.

RICHARD:
You know what gets me up in the morning?

PAUL:
Same as other blokes?

RICHARD:
My love for my job. I love my job. I like the buzz, the challenge.

PAUL:

I *hate* my job.

RICHARD:

You haven't got a job.

PAUL:

So. If I did have I'd hate it. I'm too stressed to work.

RICHARD:

Stressed? But you don't do anything!

PAUL:

Doing nothing is stressful.

RICHARD:

Then stop doing nothing and do *something*!

PAUL:

Can't be asked.

RICHARD:

You certainly seem to have skimped on the wash this morning.

PAUL:

Faint odour is there? Be glad it ain't a hot day.

RICHARD:

I am. Why don't you go shopping and get some more, and some other essentials?

PAUL:

Oh no, that's too much effort. I'm going home after this.

RICHARD:

Right.

PAUL:

I'll get a cab. I could walk but I can't be asked.

RICHARD:

You only live…five minutes walk away. How come you've got money for cabs?

PAUL:

I ain't, it's just essential you know. Got to keep money for essentials.

RICHARD:

Do you smoke?

PAUL:

Yeah.

RICHARD:

How many a day?

PAUL:
Dunno. Forty?

RICHARD:
Forty a day? You should stop and then you'd save a fortune.

PAUL:
Nah, can't be bothered.

RICHARD:
That's strange. Smoking involves more effort than not smoking. You have to lift your arm, light up…

PAUL:
Yeah, I guess. I've never looked at this that way.

RICHARD:
I know a hypnotherapist who'd…

PAUL:
Whoah there mate, no offence, but I want to *know* what I'm doing or not doing. I don't want to be in the supermarket when I start doing dog impressions.

RICHARD:
It's not a stage show.

PAUL:
Still, nah, not for me.

RICHARD:
Alright, let's look at turning your life round. You have to get motivated. I'm here to challenge your unhelpful behaviour and turn it round by making you see how unhelpful it is and making you want to change it.

PAUL:
Oh, that sounds too much like hard work to me.

RICHARD:
It is Paul. I'll be honest with you. But your wife's benefits won't keep you all forever. You need to sort this.

PAUL:
Yeah?

RICHARD:
Have you *ever* worked?

PAUL:
Nah. Well, done a bit of this and a bit of that. Got sacked.

RICHARD:
No GCSEs or anything?

PAUL:

No, so anyway I started nicking stuff.

RICHARD:

You should have done the Duke of Edinburgh's.

PAUL:

No way, the security'd be much too good.

RICHARD:

The award scheme.

PAUL:

Right. What's that then?

RICHARD:

So, you nicked stuff.

PAUL:

One day I broke into a car to nick the stereo. It was an unmarked police car and I got collared. One year in the nick, one year suspended with community service.

RICHARD:

Did you do the community service?

PAUL:
Nah. Couldn't be bothered.

RICHARD:
So?

PAUL:
Another year in prison.

RICHARD:
Did you get anything in prison?

PAUL:
Not that I want to tell you about.

RICHARD:
Qualifications? Skills?

PAUL:
Nah.

RICHARD:
Okay, so you left school with nothing. You've had one job, from which you were sacked. You got a prison term for theft, you haven't worked since and you have a wife and child.

PAUL:
Chil-dren.

RICHARD:
Children? Plural?

PAUL:
Three.

RICHARD:
I'm amazed you managed it once.

PAUL:
Well she went on top.

RICHARD:
Your family are getting by on child benefit and you and your wife's dole money?

PAUL:
Yeah. Cherub is one, Troy's three and Victoria's four.

RICHARD:
Victoria's strangely traditional compared to the others.

PAUL:
She dropped at Victoria station. Nearly got called Thameslink.

RICHARD:
Well, I think Victoria was the right choice.

PAUL:
Yeah.

RICHARD:
So, change.

PAUL:
How? My last payment's coming up next week and there's no way anyone would employ me so there's no point bothering is there. I'm okay getting by on benefits.

RICHARD:
Hard working people, like me are paying for you and your brood to loll about and do nothing. Is that right?

PAUL:
Suits me.

RICHARD:
But is it right?

PAUL:
Ain't bothered. Don't care.

RICHARD:
What I see in front of me is sloth. Pure and simple. Sloth. Sloth got you where you are today.

PAUL:
Nah, I came in a taxi.

RICHARD:
Forget the past. Use this session as a springboard to a more positive future. It just needs Faith.

PAUL:
How do you know about her?

RICHARD:
Who?

PAUL:
Faith. The prossie I use sometimes.

RICHARD:
I meant faith as in belief, not a person. You use a prossie.

PAUL:
Yeah, sometimes. If the wife's overdone it and can't open them wide enough to straddle me.

RICHARD:
Dear God!! You really are a pratt aren't you. Sorry, but I just feel I have to tell you some home truths.

PAUL:

I'm a pratt am I? Well, you're not perfect either. I mean, you're just a cheat. Life Coach? What qualifications have you got to be a life coach?

RICHARD:

Well, life experience for one thing.

PAUL:

The university of Life doesn't count mate. I mean degrees and stuff.

RICHARD:

Oh you know what a degree is?

PAUL:

Yeah.

RICHARD:

Thought about an access course?

PAUL:

No, I know how to get in and out of places. Just a job will do for now, and one that don't need too much effort.

RICHARD:

You won't get one if we don't put a CV together?

PAUL:
A C5?

RICHARD:
A CV. A Curriculum Vitae – a summary of your achievements. Ooops, you don't have any do you?

PAUL:
Nah.

RICHARD:
I'll have to do one. I doubt you can spell and I bet your grammar's terrible.

PAUL:
My gran's fine, except when she loses at Bingo and starts effing and blinding.

RICHARD:
Grammar, not your grandma. The construction of the language.

PAUL:
Oh, right.

RICHARD:
And the way you talk. You're only a few words away from "innit!"

PAUL:

I didn't come here to be told I'm useless, unemployable, and lazy and I'll never get a job. I know that already. You were meant to sort me out.

RICHARD:

I'm a life coach, not God! I can't work miracles. I need some raw material to work with. Look, let's leave it for now. I need some thinking time. Come back next week at the same time and we'll see if we can make some progress.

PAUL:

Alright. Help us up and open the door for us mate!

THE END

ENVY

Jenny (Mediator)
Jeff (Trainee – NO LINES)
Tracey and Dave (Party 1)
Pat and John (Party 2)

Robert Chantler – The Seven Deadly Sins

ENVY

Note: Three additional chairs are required and both members of each party should be seated next to each other. The layout is thus 2 chairs on the left facing slightly towards the audience, 2 chairs on the right likewise and the other 2 in the centre facing the audience, with the coffee table in front of the back two and between those on either side.

JENNY:
Now, first I have to thank you all for coming. It's nice to get you all together in one place. This joint meeting will give you the chance to each say your piece and from that we can work our way towards an agreement. You will each have two minutes to start with. During that time you will not be interrupted but then you must show the same courtesy to the other party. I will not tolerate swearing or abusive name calling. Any of that and the meeting will be terminated. Lastly, everything that is said in this meeting is confidential and stays within this room. And next to me is Jeff, and he's in training. He will be observing this meeting. Okay?

PAT:
Okay, just get on with it.

TRACEY:
Cow!

JENNY:
Um, Tracey. I said no abusive language.

TRACEY:
Abusive? That's not f...

JENNY:
Tracey.

PAT:
You can see the sort of person we're dealing with can't you Jenny.

TRACEY:
Shut it. And I suppose she's going first is she?

JENNY:
I don't know Tracey. You made the complaint so I was hoping *you* would.

TRACEY:
Right, well it all started when my Dave got this 32" TV right. Beautiful it was. £400, right Dave?

DAVE:
Yeah.

TRACEY:

Well next day, her John came home with an even bigger one. Bloody massive it was, at least 50". Flaunted it he did. He called up "Pat! Come and help us with this 50" TV!" Just so we'd hear.

JOHN:

I didn't call her for your benefit, you stupid paranoid pr…

JENNY:

John, we agreed, no interruptions.

JOHN:

I never agreed anything.

JENNY:

Carry on Tracey.

TRACEY:

Anyway, then he asked if we wanted to come round and see it. We never asked him round to see ours. Why should we? He only did it to rub our noses in it, you know. It was all, look at this, and you can do this and that etc etc. Well, when we got home, we just couldn't enjoy ours anymore because it wasn't as good as his. He spoiled our enjoyment of our TV so my Dave had to buy a bigger one. So he did. 60". Massive. It was awesome, the biggest size you could get. That night we watched this action movie on it, in widescreen. It was totally awesome. We had the sound right up, and it was near the end, about nineish, and these two came round and starting banging on the door shouting that it was too loud. I mean nine o'clock's not late.

JENNY:
And was it too loud?

DAVE:
Well, we had to have it loud to get the benefit.

JOHN:
It's a semi, not a cinema, you noisy prick!

DAVE:
Yeah, well you can shut up because we haven't finished yet. Wait till Jenny hears what *you* did.

TRACEY:
Next day, John came home in this van. Shouted up to Pat. She came out. Then two big delivery men came over in this old Escort, and carried in the biggest speakers you've ever seen in your life. A home cinema system. Each speaker was like a coffin! We thought, oh my God, what the hell are we in for?

DAVE:
Then that night, they had it going so loud, the walls were shaking. I went round there, kicked the door in and kicked the TV, and pulled the plug out while they were watching it.

JOHN:

So I went round to Dave's and did the same to his place.

JENNY:

Okay, well that was quite unnecessary. Both of you.

JOHN:

I'd like to damage *them*.

TRACEY:

Oh, you want to be violent do you, eh? Come on then!!

JENNY:

Tracey, sit down. I think you've said enough so far.

DAVE:

We're not finished yet.

JENNY:

You are for now. Pat and John?

PAT:

John worked hard for that TV. We didn't buy it because theirs was smaller. As Dave said, we didn't come round to theirs to see it. We didn't even know they had one.

TRACEY:

Liar!

JENNY:
One more outburst like that and the meeting ends.

PAT:
The truth is they saw ours was bigger by chance and took that as us envying them and wanting to one up them. They saw ours though which is why they got the biggest one you can get.

JENNY:
But then you got a bigger sound system.

PAT:
Suppose. But they started it.

TRACEY:
You started it.

PAT:
You started it.

TRACEY:
I'm not arguing about it.

PAT:
Oh not much you're not.

TRACEY:
You always want the last word don't you?

PAT:
(pause) No.

JENNY:
Pat.

PAT:
Well, John and I couldn't make them think they'd beaten us so we got the best sound system, we knew they couldn't beat it.

JENNY:
But they didn't flaunt their TV did they?

PAT:
They left the box outside so everyone could see they had one.

JENNY:
Did you Tracey?

TRACEY:
We put it out for the rubbish that's all. What do you think we'd do with it in the house, sleep in it!

JENNY:
Okay, fair point.

JOHN:
If I might take over for a minute, Pat.

PAT:
Okay.

JOHN:
We were disturbed by the noise when they got their massive set. We bought a bigger sound system to teach them that they couldn't annoy people like that without getting a taste of their own medicine. Of course, they don't like it when someone gets back at them.

JENNY:
So you bought it deliberately to blast them.

JOHN:
We were going to buy it anyway but it seemed like a good time to do it, yes.

TRACEY:
You bought it out of spite.

JOHN:
Well at least Pat and I do respectable jobs for our earnings. The tone of road went right down when you chavs moved in. Chavs, that's what you two are. You belong on a council estate, not in a nice middle class road. I mean, you're called Tracey and Dave. Need I say more.

TRACEY:

Snob. We're not scum. I worked hard to earn what we have. Running your own business isn't easy you know.

JOHN:

And how many hours a day do you spend on your back then?!

TRACEY:

What are you suggesting?

JOHN:

Never mind.

JENNY:

Right, you and John lived here first I take it.

JOHN:

Yes. Ten years.

JENNY:

How long have you been here Tracey?

TRACEY:

Two and a half years.

JOHN:
The couple that lived there before were nice. Nice well-mannered children too. But his business collapsed and he had to move away. When those two (meaning TRACEY and DAVE) moved in, we knew they'd be that sort straight away.

PAT:
We did.

DAVE:
What sort?

PAT:
Chavs.

JENNY:
Did you ever get on?

JOHN:
Not really. He had a flashy car to start with so we had to sell ours and get a flashier one.

JENNY:
Why?

JOHN:
Because we have a status to maintain in this road. We can't see our yobbo neighbours better off than us.

JENNY:

Right so basically you've both been envying each other since day one. Look how you're behaving now. Kicking doors in, kicking each other's sets, swearing at each other, deafening each other. Not to mention I suspect considerable impact on the other residents nearby.

JOHN:

Well, if they stopped flaunting their wealth, we might tone it down a bit.

JENNY:

That's a very generous concession John. Dave and Tracey, will you do the same?

DAVE:

If we must. They have to say they started it though.

JOHN:

Never. We did the decent thing and made the first move and you should do the same.

DAVE:

We didn't flaunt our set at you, you flaunted yours at us.

JOHN:

You had a flashier car.

DAVE:

I already had it before we moved in you stupid prick, I didn't buy it to one-up you.

JOHN:

Anyway, we didn't even know you had the TV. You only bought it one day before us, you hadn't even left the box out.

TRACEY:

I bet you or that nosey cow Pat saw Dave bring it in.

PAT:

Rubbish, and don't you call me a nosey cow.

JOHN:

Absolutely. You'd better be able to prove what you said.

TRACEY:

I don't.

PAT:

You do, you flash bitch!

TRACEY:

Don't call me a flash bitch!

JENNY:

Enough, enough! Dave and Tracey, will you agree not to flaunt your possessions if they don't?

TRACEY:

No, because we never did.

JENNY:

Alright, maybe these occasions were just coincidence.

TRACEY:

Yes.

JENNY:

But I'm sure you rubbed their noses in things too before now. Two years, this has been going on, so you must have done at some time. What about the car for instance?

DAVE:

I already had the car, I told you. "Tall Trees" down the end have an Aston DB9 in their drive, he ain't envying *them* is he?

JOHN:

I can't. There isn't a better car.

DAVE:

In your opinion.

JENNY:
Whoever started it in my opinion is irrelevant now. The time has come for making up. Now we can't leave here with an agreement unless both sides concede or agree on something. I thought it would not be unreasonable to get you all to agree not to flaunt each other's possessions, and you agreed, and then we had all this.

TRACEY:
Well, we won't ever be best buddies. If they stay out of our way, we'll stay out of theirs. That's the best you're going to get.

DAVE:
Yeah, and they have to admit they started it and apologise first.

JENNY:
No, neither of you are going to take responsibility for who started it. It was almost certainly six of one and half a dozen of the other.

TRACEY:
It was them. They started it.

JOHN:
It was you that started it. By moving in!

TRACEY:
We are allowed to move in. We can live where we like. We bought the house. You don't like it, tough!

PAT:
Move out. That would solve the problem.

DAVE:
Why don't you?

PAT:
We are the right sort of people for the road, and you're not. So you should go somewhere else. Like the flats over the chip shop. Where you sort should be!

JENNY:
Pat, please apologise.

PAT:
No.

JENNY:
That was unacceptable.

PAT:
No.

JOHN:
We damn well won't apologise. To people like that.

TRACEY:
People like what!?

JOHN:
People like you!

JENNY:
Alright, well you don't like each other, that's obvious. Either you both sign an agreement that you will a) stay out of each other's way, and b) stop showing off your purchases, or the meeting's over and you can just get on with it. I have never seen envy cause such trouble in all my years of mediating. It's got totally out of hand.

PAT:
Alright.

JOHN:
Alright.

TRACEY:
Suppose.

DAVE:
Suppose.

JENNY:
Good. Well I will draw up an agreement, and you both sign it. It isn't legally binding but it's good will. You sign your copy and send it back

to our office and you John and Pat, do the same. I'll follow you up in about six weeks and see how things are going. Thank you all for your time tonight.

THE END

Robert Chantler – The Seven Deadly Sins

GREED

Simon (Counsellor)
Sarah and George (Couple)

Robert Chantler – The Seven Deadly Sins

GREED

SIMON:
Hello, both of you. Please come in. You must be George and you must be Sarah.

SARAH:
Oh, you guessed that from the bosoms did you?

SIMON:
Hmmm.

GEORGE:
Ignore her. She's a rude cow.

SARAH:
What?!!!

SIMON:
Right, well let's try to be civil while we're all here shall we? Why don't you tell me what brought you here?

GEORGE:
The last straw!

SARAH:
I'll tell the story. As you're the one in the wrong.

GEORGE:
Me? You're the one at fault.

SARAH:
Shut up.

GEORGE:
Yes dear.

SARAH:
I sent George out to buy our weekly lottery ticket. When he came back and we watched the draw he was clutching the pink form that you give to the shop assistant to put in the machine and register the numbers.

SIMON:
But no ticket?

SARAH:
No. And five of our numbers came up. Bad enough it wasn't six but five numbers is still good, so I asked him to show me the ticket and he hadn't got it, so I went ape.

GEORGE:
But…

SARAH:
Shut up George, I won't tell you again.

GEORGE:
Sorry dear.

SARAH:
I had no idea he'd been so devious. I just thought it was another of his bizarre shopping trips that I blame on him for being thick!

SIMON:
What do you mean "bizarre shopping trips?"

SARAH:
Well, once I sent him down to the village to buy The Guardian and he came back with some grapefruit, another time I sent him for some single cream and he came back with crème fraiche, and last week I sent him out to buy some flour and he came back with a packet of tampons. I mean he is just so stupid!

GEORGE:
I'm not. When we went on holiday to Spain last year you bought three packs of condoms even though you've not got a willy.

SIMON:
Can we stick to the story that brought you here please?

GEORGE:
I'll tell it as Sarah seems incapable. I didn't do anything underhand. I just brought back the wrong slip.

SARAH:

Liar! I know you had the winning ticket as well but you kept it quiet so you wouldn't have to share the winnings with me.

GEORGE:

Prove it!

SARAH:

I read our bank statement. £2,500 paid in. Suspicious? I thought so.

GEORGE:

I won that on a bet.

SARAH:

But you didn't tell me.

GEORGE:

I would have got round to it.

SARAH:

Rubbish. And you never won that on a bet. The bank sent me a copy of the cheque and it was from Camelot!!

GEORGE:

You never said anything about that.

SIMON:
So, George. Did you make Sarah think you hadn't bought a ticket when you had so that you could keep the £2,500 winnings for yourself?

GEORGE:
Um...

SIMON:
It's okay George, it's okay to be honest here. Honesty is what we need all round in marriage counselling? Honesty is the key to a good marriage.

GEORGE:
You can tell you've never been married.

SARAH:
He knows he's guilty. That's why he can't say it.

GEORGE:
Alright, I did it. But then I was going to surprise you by revealing that we had won it after all.

SIMON:
But you didn't.

GEORGE:
I would have done. I was going to.

SARAH:
But you didn't.

GEORGE:
Only because before I got round to it you were such a cow, I decided – "stuff you!" My money. You'd have done the same.

SARAH:
Prove it.

GEORGE:
You've done it before. The Bingo win?

SARAH:
A hundred, that's all. Hardly two and half thousand!

GEORGE:
Two hundred.

SARAH:
So, still not even close.

SIMON:
But in fairness Sarah, you were dishonest too.

SARAH:
No.

GEORGE:

You had no intention of telling me about that Bingo win.

SARAH:

I play every week. I often win little amounts. You don't tell me every time you win on a bet.

GEORGE:

I don't win much.

SARAH:

Well, I've only got your word for that haven't I.

GEORGE:

You don't trust me.

SARAH:

No. You tried to hide £2,500 from your own wife.

GEORGE:

If you hadn't flown off the handle at me over your thinking I'd got the wrong ticket without giving me a chance to explain, I'd have told you. But as I said, you were such a cow! Anyway, if I'd wanted to hide the fact I wouldn't have put into our joint account would I. I'd have set up a separate one.

SARAH:

You're not clever enough. Besides, you never let me see the bank statements away. If I do occasionally see the odd one, it's either an accident or a miracle.

GEORGE:

She makes out like I'm always dishonest.

SARAH:

You are. What about that year when you phoned round my friends and told them to say they hadn't sent me a Christmas card while they were and you were hiding them. Another surprise you forgot to tell me about until I found them wrapped in brown paper in your underwear drawer!!

GEORGE:

Yes, well, I forgot. You shouldn't have been in my underwear drawer. I don't fumble about in your knickers.

SARAH:

Tell me about it.

SIMON:

Look, I think there is more to your marital problems than a few incidents if dishonesty, don't you agree?

SARAH:

It's greed. Greed, greed, greed!

GEORGE:
You don't have to say it three times, that's just greedy.

SARAH:
You're not funny so put a sock in it. I don't put my bingo winnings into our joint account because they always pay out in cash and it's only little amounts.

SIMON:
But you can pay small amounts into a bank account?

SARAH:
Yeah, but for small amounts it's too much hassle.

SIMON:
You should be declaring all income for tax purposes you know, both of you.

SARAH:
Not lottery wins. You pay tax when you buy the ticket!

SIMON:
Alright, well what about Bingo.

SARAH:
So?

GEORGE:

Not paying it in because it's a small amount is a pathetic excuse. See how she twists things Simon. She's like this at home too.

SARAH:

Only when you really irritate me!

GEORGE:

I meant facts not my balls.

SARAH:

It gives me no pleasure believe me, twisting your balls.

GEORGE:

Well why do you do it then? Shall I start twisting your nipples?

SARAH:

Not if you have any sense.

SIMON:

Yes, well, let's go somewhere else shall we?

GEORGE:

Yes. You cow!

SARAH:

Pig!

GEORGE:
Goat!

SIMON:
Okay, so you know the farmyard animals. Can we try and sort your marriage out?

GEORGE:
I know what would sort it out.

SIMON:
What?

GEORGE:
Divorce. She goes.

SARAH:
You go more like!

GEORGE:
You, you mean.

SIMON:
But surely if you really wanted a divorce, neither of you would be here would you?

SARAH:

Do you know, I don't remember why I even thought about coming here. I must have been drunk to have agreed. Was it your idea George?

GEORGE:

No. I didn't want to come for counselling. It's a waste of time as far as I'm concerned. If we want to slag each other with a referee I have mates who'd do that.

SIMON:

Counselling is not a waste of time. Deep down, my troubled clients are all good people who have just lost their way in their relationships and I help them see things from a neutral perspective, no siding, no blaming, just exploring and confronting.

SARAH:

I'd divorce him tomorrow.

GEORGE:

I *am* here you know, you can talk to the face!

SARAH:

Alright, I'd divorce you tomorrow.

GEORGE:

Oh, promises, promises!

SARAH:

What have you got going for you? You're thick, deceitful and not exactly Mel Gibson.

GEORGE:

Leave it out, have you looked in the mirror lately. Oh no, you can't can you, I forgot you didn't have a reflection!

SARAH:

How dare you criticise me?

GEORGE:

I tell you Simon, you wouldn't be laughing if you saw what I saw first thing in the morning.

SARAH:

I bet he would, and what's more, he'd need binoculars.

GEORGE:

I was referring to you. You look like your face had a collision with a beanbag.

SARAH:

Oh yeah, well you look like…

GEORGE:

And I don't go round like I've got a bad smell under my nose.

SARAH:

No, that's because *you* haven't. You *are* the smell.

SIMON:

Please! Can't you two see yourselves? So to speak. You're like two children! This is a very dysfunctional relationship and if you want to sort it out it's going to take a few sessions and a bit more maturity from both of you. If we can just get the greed issue sorted today that'll be a start.

SARAH:

Alright, but he has to say sorry first, and promise never to let his greed get the better of him again.

SIMON:

George?

GEORGE:

I will not. She must apologise to me. She's the worse offender.

SARAH:

I am not!

SIMON:

Okay, Sarah says she wins often on the Bingo but only small amounts and the payments are in cash and she doesn't bother banking them. You win a large amount relative to hers but you put it into your joint account. I think Sarah should apologise as she hasn't been as transparent as you, by not putting her winnings into your account.

SARAH:
Marriage counsellors aren't meant to take sides.

SIMON:
Agreed, but there is an impasse here, and if I don't weigh in, it won't be resolved. Anyway, George presumably knew you'd see the joint statement. Actually, George why did you put it into your joint account if you wanted to hide it?

GEORGE:
I had to. It was a cheque.

SIMON:
Ah, of course.

SARAH:
Oh, so if it had been cash, you wouldn't have done?

GEORGE:
I never said that.

SARAH:
You as good as did.

SIMON:
How long have you two been together?

GEORGE:
Nearly twenty years.

SARAH:
You only get fourteen for murder. And I've thought about it, believe me.

GEORGE:
Yeah, well so have I.

SARAH:
You're not bright enough to kill me.

GEORGE:
Don't rely on outward appearances.

SIMON:
Why don't you both shake hands, hug and make up. Then nobody needs to apologise first, and neither of you will lose face. And can we resolve to not hide any wins from each other in future or let greed rear it's ugly head again. It's a deadly sin you know, greed.

GEORGE:
I will if she will.

SARAH:
I will if he will.

SIMON:
I'll count you in. And then when I say "Go", you at least shake hands. Alright.

GEORGE and SARAH:
Okay.

SIMON:
One, two, three, go!!

(THEY do)

SIMON:
Hug?

GEORGE:
Leave it out!

SARAH:
Yeah, one step at a time.

SIMON:
So, you both willing to give this counselling a go then?

SARAH:

I suppose so. We're getting on a bit and haven't got that long to go so we might as well enjoy our last years.

GEORGE:

Definitely. Here's to hoping you fall off your perch first.

SARAH:

Same to you.

SIMON:

Right, see you next week. See Fanny on the way out.

GEORGE:

Oh yes, I vaguely remember that.

SIMON:

She'll take your money.

GEORGE:

Oh, your receptionist. Yes.

SARAH:

Come on. Mind you, I suppose you can't embarrass me any further.

GEORGE:

(farts)

SARAH:

Oh how wrong I was.

THE END

Robert Chantler – The Seven Deadly Sins

WRATH

Tom (Therapist)
Sam (Client)

Robert Chantler – The Seven Deadly Sins

WRATH

SAM:

I don't know why I'm here. I'm not an angry person, it's just everything really ticks me off that's all!

TOM:

Well Sam, you're here because you don't want to go to prison for a year.

SAM:

Don't patronise me. That really makes me angry!

TOM:

I thought you said you weren't an angry person.

SAM:

Well, everyone is sometimes. You must get angry yourself sometimes!

TOM:

Not at all. I practice mindfulness twice a day every day. I feel a deep sense of calm all the time, and it's wonderful.

SAM:

Right, well you've ticked me off already!

TOM:

If you'd stayed calm Sam, you wouldn't be here now and we wouldn't be having this conversation.

SAM:

Look, just do what you have to do so we can get it over with.

TOM:

It's not what I have to do Sam, it's what *you* have to do.

SAM:

What do *I* have to do?

TOM:

Convince me that you can manage your anger so you don't repeat the behaviour that led you to be here.

SAM:

What if I can't?

TOM:

Then I'll have to tell your probation officer that your therapy was unsuccessful.

SAM:

But if you do that, I'll be sent to prison for sure.

TOM:
Well, you have the ultimate incentive don't you. If you want to stay out of prison.

SAM:
When things I can't control get dumped on me I get angry. Other people make me angry, but I'm not an angry person inside. Other people make me angry.

TOM:
You're denying ownership of the feeling Sam, classic bad move. You can blame others for making you feel a certain way but you are responsible for your own actions.

SAM:
Alright, you tell me, when I've told you this, that you wouldn't have got angry, right.

TOM:
Okay.

SAM:
I was in the supermarket. I had a pint of milk and some dog food and a few bits in a basket. I had cash in my hand ready to pay. I'd found the one short queue in the store, and who do I get stuck behind?

TOM:
I don't know.

SAM:

Some silly cow faffing about with loyalty cards and coupons, and then she didn't even have enough cash so she got her credit card out and that was refused so she got out another one and that went through but then she needed her bags packed. Lazy cow, she could have packed her own bags as she went, but oh no. Ten minutes it took for me to get served and get out. I nearly dumped the stuff and stormed out.

TOM:

What did you do?

SAM:

I tapped her on the shoulder. She turned round. I said "Oy, some of us don't want to be here at closing time you stupid cow. Shift yourself!"

TOM:

That wasn't very nice.

SAM:

She asked for it. Anyway, she got the hump and started telling me to mind my own business. Well, I wasn't having that. So I got the bread out of my basket and smacked her on the head with it.

TOM:

Anger?

SAM:
Frustration.

TOM:
Anger.

SAM:
Justice.

TOM:
You can't say the word, can you! You're in such denial you can't even accept you get angry.

SAM:
I SAID I GET ANGRY!! I said that!! Sometimes, we all do. I know you say you don't, but I bet you do. Where is this therapy I'm supposed to be having? Seems you're just making me recount stories that are bound to make me angry so you can write a bad report saying I'm angry and that is not acceptable and I'm angry about that! (sudden pause) I mean, I'm not angry about that, I'm…I'm…displeased. Displeased is what I am.

TOM:
You're here because you punched a motorist in the face for hooting you after you overtook him on the inside, which is illegal and which was witnessed.

SAM:
So, he shouldn't have hooted me. I hate people hooting me. I've got a bumper sticker that says "If you hoot me, I'll kill you" and another one that says "How's My Driving? Who gives a f***"

TOM:
More signs of aggression. How have you shown me so far that you'd be able to manage your anger?

SAM:
That's your job to help me to manage this anger I'm meant to have.

TOM:
Not "meant to have," "do have"

SAM:
Alright, I'm angry. Alright, will that shut you up? I'm angry, okay!

TOM:
Good, well owning your feelings is the first important step towards treatment.

SAM:
You sound like a counsellor.

TOM:
Well, thanks Sam, because I am one, as it happens.

SAM:

Have you got out of your armchair and seen the real world? Sometimes I just want to scream, and just...explode. Everyone does. You're like, treating me like I'm the only person who's ever punched anyone in the face.

TOM:

Let me ask you a question, Sam. What purpose is served by getting angry?

SAM:

It makes me feel better.

TOM:

Okay. How else could you make yourself feel better?

SAM:

A wank?

TOM:

When you feel yourself getting angry.

SAM:

A drink.

TOM:

Could you do something more constructive?

SAM:
Lego?

TOM:
Something socially useful. Something to make you feel good about yourself. Something creative.

SAM:
Creative? What planet are you from? I've not got an original thought in my head.

TOM:
Or very much at all.

SAM:
What?

TOM:
Nothing. You must have some talents. I know it's hard to find the milk when the supermarket shelves are empty but dig deep.

SAM:
Why, do they keep it underground?

TOM:
It's a metaphor, Sam.

SAM:

Yeah, whatever. Look, stop with the fancy words and tell me what to do, if you're such an expert.

TOM:

Well, okay, next time you start to feel angry, take a few deep breaths, in and out and just smile, and tell yourself all the anger you were feeling has all gone.

SAM:

That won't work.

TOM:

How do you know?

SAM:

Because it won't. Deep breathing!? If that's the best you can do...

TOM:

You'd better try anything going Sam because you're not here voluntarily. You're here to stay out of prison. What better incentive could there be for trying something new.

SAM:

Stop bringing that up!! Stop rubbing my nose in it!! What's the matter with you, can't you see it winds me up!

TOM:
I only mentioned it twice. That shouldn't make you angry. At the slightest provocation, you're ready to blow.

SAM:
After a big kebab I often do.

TOM:
You haven't had a big kebab before coming here have you?

SAM:
No. Just a chile burger!

TOM:
What?

SAM:
Got you worried then, eh?

TOM:
(coughs) It's not good for your health, to get angry.

SAM:
Yeah, well. You only live once. Anyway, I wouldn't get angry if people didn't make me.

TOM:

You know, in Buddhism, it is said that you are not angry, but "with anger" and therefore you can choose to be "without anger". If anger is hitching a lift, chuck it off. That's it, in a nutshell. That way you can acknowledge it's with you but it can't become part of you. Of course we all get angry sometimes, but we diffuse it by other ways. I've been cut up by motorists. I've sat in the cab and had a good swear. But I don't hoot and flash the guy, or run him off the road and punch him in the face. I don't go home and kick the dog. I behave like a normal, civilised person.

SAM:
You saying I'm not?

TOM:
Yes.

SAM:
You can't say that to me!

TOM:
Why not?

SAM:
You looking for a slap, are you!! (pause) Sorry, not angry. Just...

TOM:
Anger is a sin, Sam, and a very grave sin. You need to control it or it will control you. One session won't be anywhere near long enough for you to sort your issues out. They must go back a long way. It seems they do.

SAM:
So?

TOM:
Let's look at some of the times you've been angry before. See if there's a pattern.

SAM:
Okay.

TOM:
When was the first time you remember getting angry?

SAM:
I don't know. Loads of times.

TOM:
Hmm.

SAM:

You've been scribbling away all the time. What you writing about me? Have you written that I'm mental? Have you? Because I'm not, and if you think I am, you're the mental one, not me!

TOM;

I'm just taking a few notes to help remind me of what you're telling me.

SAM:

Show me what you've said about me!

TOM:

There you are.

SAM:

(browses, mumbling to himself) Alright. Here.

TOM:

Thank you.

SAM:

I don't know when I first got angry, alright. But if you want a few stories, I've got loads of them. Last month, this fat cow in the supermarket. Coupons, storecards, then some of her items wouldn't go through the scanner, then they had to call a supervisor, then when she finally got round to paying, her card was rejected so she faffed around in her purse and started paying in change. If I'd been right behind her I'd have wrung her bloody neck!!

TOM:
There you go again. You can't even relate a story without blowing up.

SAM:
Well, wouldn't *you* have got angry?

TOM:
Yes, but I'd take a few deep breaths and calm myself down.

SAM:
See, I would have punched her.

TOM:
Two different ways of coping. Mine is legal and healthy, yours is illegal and unhealthy. You have a choice. We can all choose how we feel, how we react, how we behave.

SAM:
Yeah, and I choose ANGER!!!

TOM:
Well, then I guess you've made your choice. I think you'll be in the nick this time tomorrow.

SAM:
You say anything bad about me and you're next!!!

TOM:
I worked with anger management for the police for years Sam. You don't scare me. Sit down and shut up, or you'll get another couple of years for assault too.

SAM:
Some therapist you are!

TOM:
No, I'm a good therapist, it's just you're a hopeless case!

SAM:
That's it, keep the labels coming. Angry, hopeless.

TOM:
Look, with time and effort, we might make progress, but for this session, I think we've gone as far as we can go. I won't put any reports in today as long as you agree to have another session next week and then we'll see what happens. That's the offer. Take it or leave it.

SAM:
Ain't got much choice have I?

TOM:
No.

SAM:
Alright. But I'm coming under protest.

TOM:
Fine. Sign out at reception when you go.

SAM:
Yeah, whatever!

(HE slams the door)

TOM:
Such anger!! I don't think this treatment is going to have a good outcome, do you?

THE END

GLUTTONY

Steven (Counsellor – overweight)
Fred (Client – overweight)

Robert Chantler – The Seven Deadly Sins

GLUTTONY

STEVEN:
Hello Fred, come in.

FRED:
(struggles in and into chair) Well, here's a turn up for the books. You're fatter than me! Your shadow must weigh ten stone, and you're counselling *me*! Am I meant to feel better being counselled by someone fatter than me, is that the plan?

STEVEN:
Oh don't. It's not my fault I'm fat. Sitting in this chair all day listening to people like you. No offence.

FRED:
Oh, none taken.

STEVEN:
Now, you're here because you're depressed because you're too fat to work, yes?

FRED:
Yes.

STEVEN:
Well don't despair. I'm half as big again and I've got a job.

FRED:
Sitting in a chair talking to people all day. I could do that.

STEVEN:
If you had a counselling qualification, yes, you probably could.

FRED:
How can you be so fat and not mind?

STEVEN:
I do mind.

FRED:
It's just that it's all very well my doctor going on about buying organic this and organic that and fresh fruit and vegetables and all this healthy stuff but I don't have his salary and healthy stuff costs!

STEVEN:
Oh, tell me about it. I'd rather have those Mr Chubby Oven Ready Chips…

FRED:
Oh yeah.

STEVEN:
I agree with you about the cost. Why can't this healthy food be cheaper?

FRED:
Exactly.

STEVEN:
Okay, I can afford it on what I earn, but I'd rather be done at the local spending my money and then have a nice curry and chips.

FRED:
Anyway, if I could afford it I wouldn't want it. It's the sort of thing you feed your rabbit – lettuce leaves, seeds and…mung beans. I don't want to turn into one of those skinny veggies farting all the time. I enjoy my food and if I want to stuff myself stupid, why shouldn't I?

STEVEN:
Yes, but if you came here for counselling because your weight makes you depressed, why would you want to take that attitude?

FRED:
I want my lifestyle but I also want to be slimmer. Look at me, I've got more chins than a Chinese phone book. What could *I* do for a job? Be covered in Velcro and rolled around an office carpet to get the fluff off it!

STEVEN:
Mmm, that *could* work.

FRED:
Shut up!

STEVEN:
Anyway, you can't expect to be slimmer and maintain your current lifestyle, no more than I can.

FRED:
You sound like you don't want to change.

STEVEN:
Well, maybe I don't. Listen, you didn't come here to be counselled to lose weight. You came here for help with your depression.

FRED:
Yes, caused by being fat. I came here to lose weight. Yes, I'm depressed – my doctor told me if I didn't lose weight I'd be dead within the year.

STEVEN:
Mmm, depressing.

FRED:
Oh, you think? Glad all that book knowledge hasn't gone to waste. Anyway, I don't want to get old. Sucking mashed potato and fish through my gums 'cos all my teeth have fallen out and having my bum wiped by some teenage care worker.

STEVEN:
Well then, carry on stuffing and kill yourself then.

FRED:
Nice.

STEVEN:
Look, I'm fatter than you and my doctor hasn't said *I've* got a year to live. Okay, he nags me about my weight, especially now I have Diabetes and Angina but he didn't give me a death date.

FRED:
Well, shouldn't you change your attitude too?

STEVEN:
It's too late for me. I can't change. Everything's sedentary, even my job. I can hardly walk anywhere anyway I'm so fat so how am I meant to lose weight? I can hardly sleep there's so much weight on my lungs. I have an oxygen cylinder by the bed for Christ's sake. Still, you only live once and as you say, why not enjoy myself now and die young so I don't end up sucking mashed whatever you said through my gums. At least you're still getting about.

FRED:
I don't have a car. I can't fit. I have to call one of these high taxis for disabled people. I'm so hot all the time, and I can hardly breathe when I walk and I'm confused and depressed, and it sounds like you are too, which is a bummer because I came to you for you to help *me*.

STEVEN:
Okay, who am I kidding? I'm depressed. I only do this job because hearing people with worse lives than me cheers me up a little. Do you know how many clients I have whinging about this and that while they're skinny as rakes? How I have longed for this day when someone like you walks in for counselling. I'm not happy with my life. It's all an act, a professional mask. I wish I could turn away from a life of pints and fry ups but I can't.

FRED:
Me too. But still, you're supposed to be in professional mode now and be helping *me*.

STEVEN:
Yes, but I need help too. Seeing you has just made me realise how much I need help. I start eating and I can't stop. I stuff my face at breakfast. I stuff my face at brunch. I stuff my face at lunch. Then it's afternoon tea, high tea, dinner and supper. I spend so much time eating it's a wonder I have time to take dumps.

FRED:
That's no life is it?

STEVEN:
No, not really.

FRED:

I mean my doctor might be wrong about me dying in a year, but I'm not going to get anywhere with you am I. You're more depressed than me, and twice the size. I don't feel so fat now having seen you. You know, in a weird way, this has actually helped. I've got a long way to go yet and I'm nowhere near the end if you're anything to go by.

STEVEN:
Oh thanks.

FRED:
Being fat has cost me everything. It cost me my marriage, I have to use prostitutes for sex because nobody else would even think about it. I can't even have a wank because I can't reach my own willy. People would rather marry convicted killers than fat people like me. I look on the Internet and get more depressed…

STEVEN:
Don't do that. Reading about medical things on the Internet is a bad idea.

FRED:
Well if I'm going to die, I might as well die from something exciting.

STEVEN:
Doctors can be wrong you know.

FRED:
I suppose so.

STEVEN:
Maybe he just said that to try to frighten you into losing weight.

FRED:
That's not very ethical.

STEVEN:
Even if some people of our size die, it doesn't mean we all will does it. Some people smoke all their lives and live 'til a hundred and other really fit healthy people drop dead in their twenties.

FRED:
True, my dad smoked all his life and he was 80 when he died.

STEVEN:
I'm glad to hear it. That he made 80 not that he died.

FRED:
I have to ask you a question, it's really bothering me

.

STEVEN:
What's bothering you?

FRED:
Who's counselling who here?

STEVEN:
What do you mean?

FRED:
Well, it seems you're using me to feel better about yourself.

STEVEN:
So are you. Using me to feel better about *your*self.

FRED:
I'm allowed to use you to feel better about myself. I'm the one being counselled. Supposed to be anyway.

STEVEN:
Oh no! What sort of counsellor am I?

FRED:
A good one.

STEVEN:
A fat one. A bad one.

FRED:
You haven't lectured me. You're the first healthcare professional who hasn't. You've let me formulate my own ideas and thoughts. Don't put yourself down.

STEVEN:
How can I counsel you and tell you to lose weight when I'm just as bad and worse?

FRED:
Look...

STEVEN:
No, Fred. I can't continue counselling you. Gluttony is a sin, and I'm encouraging you.

FRED:
We're helping each other.

STEVEN:
Okay. Look, I know someone who is very slim, very outspoken and just the sort of person who'd be at home running a boot camp for fatties. If he saw you, he'd have you on a fitness regime that would make the Marines shake with fear.

FRED:
You haven't seen him then?

STEVEN:
Oh no way. If starvation and exertion are the only ways to lose weight I'll stay fat, thank you very much.

FRED:
Is our session over then?

STEVEN:
Yes. I'm afraid it is.

FRED:
But all we've done is console each other and justify to each other what we're doing wrong. I haven't changed at all.

STEVEN:
Nor have I. There are worse things than being fat.

FRED:
Well I'm glad my counselling helped you. I'm still depressed, and I'm still fat and none the wiser. Refer me to your friend if you like, but I think it's best if we don't see each other again.

STEVEN:
Okay.

FRED:
We can still be friends.

STEVEN:
Okay, but we just won't see each other again.

FRED:

Well, if I see you in Sunbury Tesco pushing a trolley laden with stuff through the wide aisle. I'll give you a shout.

STEVEN:

Fair enough.

FRED:

Hang on. I'd forgotten I'd come here because I needed to lose weight to work. So busy indulging in mutual moaning and denial.

STEVEN:

I haven't charged you.

FRED:

I should bloody well hope not.

STEVEN:

I can't advise you. How can I when I'm as bad as you.? Depressed but too scared to admit it, and so fat this is probably the only job I *could* do. Why don't you go and get some counselling training and set up? You could run support groups. People'd pay for that. You can do most courses by distance learning on the Internet. You only have to turn up every few months for a workshop.

FRED:

Will they take me this fat?

STEVEN:

They have to. They can't discriminate. The Disability Discrimination Act remember. The fatty's new best friend. I was twenty stone when I started training.

FRED:

What are you now?

STEVEN:

Forty stone.

FRED:

I'm only twenty two stone.

STEVEN:

Well then, there you go. It will help you get a better insight into your mind, you'll probably get some free counselling out of it from someone who doesn't have my problems and things might work out okay for you.

FRED:

Yeah, you're right. If things work out and I've got something real to live for, I might try and ditch the gluttony.

STEVEN:

So we'll still agree not to see each other professionally again?

FRED:

I think that will be best.

STEVEN:

Good luck.

FRED:

You too. Bye.

THE END

PRIDE

Helen (Therapist)
Portia (Client)

Robert Chantler – The Seven Deadly Sins

PRIDE

PORTIA:
(door flung open in theatrical manner as PORTIA enters)
Good morning, you must be Helen.

HELEN:
Yes, I am. You *must* be Portia.

PORTIA:
I am. You may curtsey and genuflect wildly now.

HELEN:
(taken aback) Why would I do that?

PORTIA:
Because, darling, I am Portia Mercedes, the Goddess of daytime television. (screams) That's why!!!

HELEN:
Oh, well I do apologise. I don't generally watch daytime television because *I* have a life!

PORTIA:
Well, I'm not used to being insulted and I don't like it.   I came here for support, to hear that I *am* wonderful and not at all like Jennifer Gold said. I suppose you haven't heard of *her* either.

HELEN:
Oh yes, the entertainment critic. She has that show on the radio. I listen sometimes. She can be really funny sometimes.

PORTIA:
(hysterical) She's mean! She said (sniffling), that I was, and I quote her words like a dagger embedded in my heart – "a shallow, vacuous no-talent with a smile like a toothpaste commercial."

HELEN:
Oh no. (tries to stifle laugh) That's terrible.

PORTIA:
Do you know how much fan mail I get? Do you?!!

HELEN:
No.

PORTIA:
Enough to be able to employ a full-time secretary to answer it all. Well, they get a signed photograph of me at my most beautiful.

HELEN:
Lovely.

PORTIA:

And I *am* beautiful. As beautiful as the legendary beauty, Helen of Troy and more beautiful still. As gorgeous as Aphrodite one hundred times over. In short, darling, a Goddess! A Queen! A prima donna!

HELEN:

I agree with you there.

PORTIA:

Oh, thank you. I misjudged you. I thought you were a sarcastic stuck up, *terrible* therapist.

HELEN:

I am.

PORTIA:

Fine, darling, fine. As long as you treat *me* like a Goddess, I'm happy.

HELEN:

Did you come here because of the bad review that Jennifer whats-her-name gave you? One person in the world doesn't think the sun shines out of your...and you're driven to therapy? You must have a really thin skin. I expect legions of cosmetic surgeons have had most of it.

PORTIA:

What?!

HELEN:
Nothing.

PORTIA:
I can't be disliked by anyone, darling. I was born to be loved. I want everyone to love me, every single person in the whole world. I just want...adoration!!

HELEN:
Well, we'd all like that but that's just not realistic now, is it?

PORTIA:
Yes, yes, yes!! It IS realistic. For people of my brilliance and fabulousness, it IS realistic. Oh, I was born to be on television. I love my audience. I love being me. (crying hysterically) I can't cope with rejection by even...one...person. (theatrical sigh) Oh, my life is over. I can't go on. (collapses into chair)

HELEN:
I expect you will though.

PORTIA:
(meaning her bosoms) These weren't cheap you know! I had Italy's finest cosmetic surgeon working on these breasts! They're magnificent. Touch them, darling, feel for yourself, feel them!!

HELEN:

No, I...I won't, thank you. But yes they really are...(sarcastic) I wish I had breasts like those.

PORTIA:

Keep wishing darling.

HELEN:

Portia. You have enough money to have anything you want, don't you.

PORTIA:

Millions! TV work, acting, modelling, photo shoots and soon, my autobiography.

HELEN:

You can write?

PORTIA:

No, ghost writer sweetie.

HELEN:

Has what Jennifer said about you changed anything?

PORTIA:

Yes.

HELEN:
You're still on TV, unfortunately. You still get modelling work?

PORTIA:
I'm in Paris next week on a shoot for Vogue.

HELEN:
Do you think your legions of fans care what Jennifer Gold says?

PORTIA:
But even if *one* person does, it means I am less than perfect. (starts to hyperventilate) I can't cope with that. Oh God, I can't breathe!

HELEN:
Okay, okay. Use this. (hands her a paper bag)

PORTIA:
Over my head?

HELEN:
I wish. No, hold it over your mouth and nose, and breathe nice and slowly.

PORTIA:
(starts to calm down) I'm okay now. I'm okay.

HELEN:
Oh joy.

PORTIA:
But not to be liked is the end of my world.

HELEN:
It's one review, Portia. One bad review, out of how many? Hundreds?

PORTIA:
One too many.

HELEN:
It's not realistic to expect every single person to like you?

PORTIA:
But I *want* that!

HELEN:
Because you're spoilt!

PORTIA:
I know!!! (deep fast exhaling – calms down) But I like being spoilt.

HELEN:
What if you were left penniless one day? What will you do when you get older and you lose your youthful good looks?

PORTIA:
I haven't thought about that. I would kill myself darling. (she rushes to the window and opens it, and goes to climb out) I'll jump!! I will, and don't try and stop me.

HELEN:
I won't. The room's on the ground floor.

PORTIA:
Damn it!!! I'm a failure! Jennifer was right. Oh God, I can't bear it. (slumps into chair with head in hands, sobbing)

HELEN:
Portia?

PORTIA:
Go away!!

HELEN:
Portia.

PORTIA:
My life is over!!

HELEN:
Sadly that's not true. Your life is not over unless you want it to be. You've still got your fans, your money, your fame. What can one bad review do to change that?

PORTIA:
It's Jennifer Gold. Not any old critic darling. She is to critics what I am to stars!!

HELEN:
Still...

PORTIA:
I'll kill her. I'll do it. That'll teach her not to write bad things about me. I'll take a quill pen and plunge it through her heart!!

HELEN:
And go to prison?

PORTIA:
I wouldn't go to prison. I'm famous!

HELEN:
Yes, I suppose all those other celebrities have just been unlucky.

PORTIA:
So, alright, maybe I wouldn't kill her. So I love myself, I have pride. What's wrong with that?

HELEN:
Nothing. But it must be tempered with humility. Pride can be a sin when taken to excess; humility is a virtue. Fame and humility *can* go together you know. You could be just as famous and just as beautiful, but be a nicer person inside.

PORTIA:
I don't buy that. Give me one example of a humble *and* famous person?

HELEN:
Mother Theresa. The Dalai Lama...

PORTIA:
But are they rich?

HELEN:
No, but money isn't everything.

PORTIA:
It *is* darling. Luxury, comfort – that was my destiny. This package (gesturing to her body) was not made to rough it!

HELEN:
Have you ever seen a psychiatrist?

PORTIA:

I have my own analyst. I had a psychiatrist to but I sacked him for daring to tell me I was histrionic, even borderline. Can you believe that? Like Glen Close in Fatal Attraction he said!

HELEN:

Ah.

PORTIA:

My analyst has never said I am anything other than perfect. He once looked me straight in the eyes and said he was my number one fan.

HELEN:

Oh, a charlatan then.

PORTIA:

No darling, he's absolutely genuine. He just knows if he wants my continued business he'd better tow the line.

HELEN:

Whatever makes you happy.

PORTIA:

Can I just talk about myself now? I need to talk about me.

HELEN:

Talk about anything you like, it's still £100 an hour.

PORTIA:
I was destined for stardom you know. I was on stage when I was still in nappies. I was in baby photo competitions, school plays, photo shoots. I was born to be exposed. My parents spotted my talents and pushed me all the way. I went to RADA you know darling, RADA, not any old stage school. I've mingled with A-list celebrities, been to all the top parties, drunk myself stupid, snorted cocaine…the works, darling. I am a star. I am a goddess!!

HELEN:
You *are* an airhead.

PORTIA:
What-ever!!

HELEN:
Oh God. I want to jump, but I can't because we're on the ground floor. *You* could, because you'd keep going.

PORTIA:
Where?

HELEN:
To Hell.

PORTIA:
Ouch sweetie.

HELEN:
So far, in my opinion as a therapist, I have made some initial observations. You're vain. You're shallow. You're self obsessed and totally obnoxious. All this "sweetie, darling" rubbish is as fake as your tan! You come crying to counselling because you think you're so wonderful then you prattle on about how fabulous you are and leave *me* wanting to cry – what kind of a monster are you?!

PORTIA:
Ouch, darling!

HELEN:
Truth hurts Portia, but it's for your own good. You must embrace humility or be totally engulfed in the very vacuousness that Jennifer said you had. You have a lot going for you, but I won't list any things because you'll be off on one again. Just be a bit more humble, make some time for others, and you'll be better off for it, I promise.

PORTIA:
Humility doesn't get you to the top of your game.

HELEN:
But you're not at the top of your game. Okay, you've done some modelling and a few photo shoots...

PORTIA:
Vogue, darling. (pause) Vogue.

HELEN:

Whatever. Oh God, now I'm even starting to talk like you! Help!!! (pause) What I'm trying to say is that you're just a breakfast TV presenter, not...Julia Roberts. A third of the country are still in bed when you're on TV, a third couldn't give a damn, and the other third are so bleary eyed, King Kong could be hosting the show for all they cared. Get your life in perspective!!

PORTIA:

You're mean!! Have your hundred pounds. Dream about earning that sort of money every minute. When you're twenty thousand pounds richer every time you get up, when your picture is all over the world, when you're on national television and look a million dollars, then maybe, maybe you'll have the right to find fault. But I didn't come here to be put down.

HELEN:

Didn't you? Oh well, you have been now.

PORTIA:

I have too strong an ego to take on board your drivel. You're possessed. You're The Devil!! Jump out of the window darling and you'll be express-wayed down there. Old Nick'll have his fork up that tight arse of yours before you can blink!! (she storms out)

HELEN:
This has been the hardest hundred pounds I've ever earned. See you same time next week then?

PORTIA:
Before I go, let me just check my mirror. (screams) Aaaghhh!

HELEN:
What?!

PORTIA:
A blemish! On my nose. It's like…Comic Relief or something. It must have just come up. This is your fault, making me stressed. Do something!

HELEN:
I can hardly see it. If you hadn't said anything I wouldn't have noticed. Put a bit of spot gel on it. What do you want me to do about it? I'm a counsellor. Not a dermatologist.

PORTIA:
I look awful!

HELEN:
You look fine.

PORTIA:
Don't lie.

HELEN:
Alright, you look terrible.

PORTIA:
Oh, I am wounded. You viper in my bosom!!

HELEN:
It's fine.

PORTIA:
I might get more!

HELEN:
Yes.

PORTIA:
Oh my God!!

HELEN:
But chances are you won't.

PORTIA:
Have you a client's washroom?

HELEN:
Through reception.

PORTIA:

A little make up on that before I even leave your surgery!

HELEN:

You can pay on the way out.

PORTIA:

Huh!! (door slams)

HELEN:

God, she is something else. (sighs) Pride, vanity – sins indeed.

THE END

Robert Chantler – The Seven Deadly Sins

Robert Chantler – The Seven Deadly Sins

Robert Chantler – The Seven Deadly Sins

www.ingramcontent.com/pod-product-compliance
Lightning Source LLC
Chambersburg PA
CBHW071215160426
43196CB00012B/2315